Easy
Business
Success

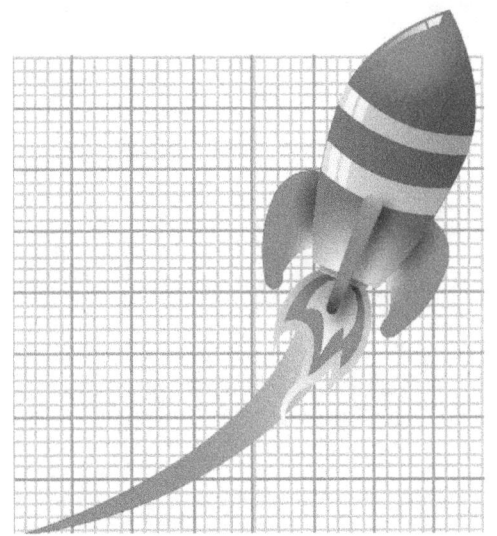

By an Expert with 25 Years Experience

35 easy to read tips

Easy Business Success Tips For All Types Of businesses-35 easy to read tips.

Busy business men and women have not got time to read a lot of pages of stuff. So we have kept the tips short and sweet.

These tips will definitely help your business succeed if you **practice** them. Take one tip a week put it into practice **before going on to the next one.**

It is the **practice** that counts, then your business truly abounds, as do you.

This guide teaches you to be the KING/QUEEN of the market place.

It is written for you, to solve your business problems and help you succeed and grow. Anything simple is very powerful. So please do not underestimate the amazing power of the book to help you succeed.

Boost your business and life now.

We are **dedicated** to saving you money, time and worry.

Some tips are repeated for reinforcement purposes.

<u>Business Success</u> 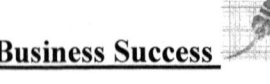 **<u>Tip 1:</u>**

Without creating **trust** with your customers and clients you have no business.

Business success 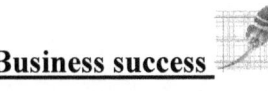 **Tip 2:**

Obtaining **customer trust** through **totally honourable** dealings is most important to your business success.

Business success 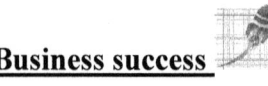 **Tip 3:**

Faith in yourself is the most important key. Why is this so?

<u>Business success</u> 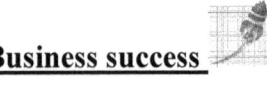 **<u>Tip 4:</u>**

Why is faith in yourself is the most important key? Yes you have guessed it.
Why should anyone have faith in you if you do not?

The next obvious step is: Have **faith in your product or service**.

Business success 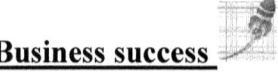 Tip 5:

Yes you have guessed it: if you do not have faith in your goods and services, why should anyone else?

Business success 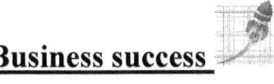 Tip 6:

What is a very important key to business success?

Enjoy and love the work you do in your business and you are bound to be successful: This person set up a very small jewellery shop during recession in a very small area. He has big high street names as his competitors. He loves and enjoys his work. He is phenomenally successful.

Business success 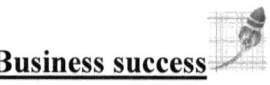 Tip 7:

Regenerate often providing free training. Please ring 0800 6122029. There are free innovation grants are available as well in the form of vouchers. Most councils provide free training. I know WLDC provide that. One can get a lot of free training on You tube.

On You tube you will get some people giving excellent training which is easy to learn and follow, as everything is laid out. But a lot of it is not so good. So one has to keep trying, till one finds the good one. Good ones are there and not too difficult to find if you persist.

<u>Business success</u>   <u>Tip 8:</u>

6 Bookkeeping Tips:

Accurate Bookkeeping is **totally essential** to business success.

Most businesses want to do bookkeeping themselves to save costs. This is understandable. However, most of the bookkeeping has huge errors in it. This is because most businesses get no advice from accountants who take the view that it is not their problem, as they are not doing the bookkeeping. This is a wrong attitude in our view. In the next few tips we will provide guidance through our tips on how it should be done properly. It has now become even more important to do it perfectly as HMRC now impose hefty penalties even for small errors.

The first tip is: most people who do bookkeeping on spreadsheets or manually have the headings on the left hand side. It is better to have the headings on the top of the columns with totals at the bottom of each sales or expense heading.

For example:
£

Date	Sales	Motoring	Cost Of Sales	General Expenses
5/1/13	6500	49	676	201

Total for month
Total from last month
Total CFwd

The above headings are only an example of the type of headings you can use. Please use other headings that you need (but do not use too many).

Your accountant only wants the totals for the year of sales and each expense heading. Keep the **list** of expense headings **short**. For example, General expenses heading can be used for many types of expenses eg business insurance, stationary etc.

Use one page for cash expenses and a separate one for bank expenses for each month. This makes it easy to reconcile the bank each month.

Business success 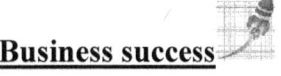 **Tip 9:**

The SECOND bookkeeping tip is : Please write the cheque number on the top of all invoices or cash if you pay by cash. If you paid by credit card please write CC. This will make the bookkeeping easier for you.

Business success 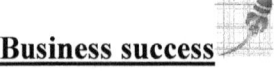 **Tip 10:**

The Third Bookkeeping Tip is: The last tip, makes it easy to **reconcile** the **bank** so make sure it is done for **every month**.

Business success  Tip 11:

The Fourth Bookkeeping tip is: To begin with have 2 folders for all your bills: one for customers and one for suppliers. When customers have paid you or you have paid your creditors, transfer invoices into the 3rd and 4th PAID folders. Then the remaining unpaid bills are your debtors and creditors at any given time. Hence in total, you should have 4 folders: 2 for paid invoices and 2 for unpaid invoices (debtors or creditors).

<u>Business success</u>   **<u>Tip 12:</u>**

The Fifth bookkeeping tip is:

Business records you may need to keep:

1. Keep a Record for all sales and other business receipts preferably as they come in.
2. Record all purchases as they arise.
3. Record all other expenses as they arise.
4. Keep a record of all purchases and sales of assets used in your business.
5. Record all amounts taken out of the business for your own or your family's personal use either in cash or withdrawn from the business bank account.
6. Record all amounts paid into the business from personal funds.
7. Keep supporting records, for example, receipts, invoices, bank statements and paying-in slips to show where the income came from and expenses were incurred. HMRC wants evidence of everything.
8. HMRC have now started a records check. If the records are not kept properly and hence the bookkeeping not done properly HMRC can fine you up to £3000.

Please remember that sales include:

1. Goods taken from stock for your own, or your family's use, that are not paid for in cash.
2. Goods or services supplied to someone else in exchange for goods or services.

Business success **Tip 13:**

The 6TH Bookkeeping and also **business success** tip: **Simplify!**

6 Bookkeeping Tips Summarised. Bookkeeping is so Important for business success we have repeated it:

The first tip is: most people who do bookkeeping on spreadsheets or manually have the headings on the left hand side. It is better to have the headings on the top of the columns with totals at the bottom of each sales or expense heading as shown in tip 8.
The SECOND tip is : Please write cheque number on all invoices or cash if you pay by cash. If you paid by credit card please write CC. This will make the bookkeeping easier for you.
The Third tip is: The last tip makes it easy to reconcile the bank so make sure it is done for every month.
The Fourth Bookkeeping tip is: To begin with have 2 folders for all your bills, one for customers and one for suppliers. When customers have paid you or you have paid your creditors, transfer invoices into the 3rd and 4th PAID folders. Then the remaining unpaid bills are your debtors and creditors at any given time. Hence in total, you should have 4 folders.
Fifth bookkeeping tip is:
Business records you may need to keep:

- Record all sales and other business receipts preferably as they come in
- Record all purchases as they arise
- Record all other expenses as they arise
- Keep a record of all purchases and sales of assets used in your business
- Record all amounts taken out of the business for your own or your family's personal use either in cash or withdrawn from the business bank account
- Record all amounts paid into the business from personal funds
- Keep supporting records, for example, receipts, invoices, bank statements and paying-in slips to show where the income came from.

HMRC have now started a records check. If the records are not kept properly and the hence the bookkeeping not done properly, HMRC can fine you up to £3000.

Please remember that sales include:

Goods taken from stock for your own, or your family's use that are not paid for in cash.
Goods or services supplied to someone else in exchange for goods or services.

6TH Bookkeeping and business tip: Simplify!

Business success **tip 15:**

10 Keys To Success

1. Before one can plan, one needs to know what one wants to do.
2. So first you have to decide what business you want to go in.
3. Then you have to decide is what people want from your chosen business.
4. Who, what, where, when.
5. The next step is to have quantifiable a goal with dates to achieve it by: ie how much money you want to earn by what date?
7. Then one can plan.
8. All this needs to be written down.
9. Then action. It has to be systemised and written down.
10. Then success!

Ask other people in business to give their experiences. When we all share we all learn more. You can do so by joining the business success group and advertise your business free for life:
http://www.facebook.com/groups/306912652690200/
If this link does not work copy and paste it on the search bar.

Business Success    Tip 16:

Always try to obtain customer feedback/complaints to grow your business. Have a small card by the till to give to customers (or email) asking for feedback. Keep it short and simple:

1. Did you get value for money: fair   good   excellent

2. Was the service friendly: fair   good   excellent

3. Would you recommend us to family/friends: yes / no

4. Please make any suggestions you may have: ------------------------
----

----

5. If you have a complaint please write it there so we can rectify your concerns: ---
----

<u>Business success</u> 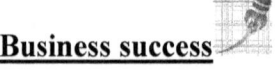 **<u>Tip17:</u>**

The customer is KING/QUEEN: By treating customers **well** businesses increase chances of succeeding.

Business Success 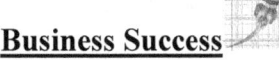 Tip 18:

Take initiative to market your business as marketing is the **lifeblood** of your business. Use **all** channels of marketing. Marketing effort is never wasted: We once gave a card to a photographer. After 2 years he recommended me to a printer who remained our client for many years till he retired.

Free channels of marketing: Face book (join business groups), twitter (follow businesses and they follow you back), Linked in, Business Biscotti, Google Maps, You Tube etc. Give them free tips on how to use your products/services to solve their problems.

Low cost channels: web site, business cards, leaflets, Google ad words (set a daily spend limit) etc

Expensive channels: Newspaper and magazine advertising etc.

The Most Effective Channel is: Customer recommendation. They stay with you for a long time. Also Net working (not online) is quite effective. There are many networking groups (Google them). Ask your existing customers to recommend you by offering a discount for every recommendation for the next purchase.

Success of each type of channel depends on the type of business you are in and on your content.

Business Success 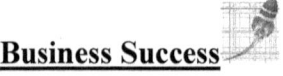 **Tip 19**: For rented property businesses:

Do all landlords know that the deposit has to be lodged with the DPS (there is also an insurance backed option). The DPS expect, a third party going in and preparing an exit inventory, preferably with photographs, or better still with a video. We recommend the **video option** as it misses very little and provides a much better proof.

Business Success  **Tip 20:**

It is the **practice** that counts then your business truly abounds, as do you: Have you put into **practice** all the business success tips we have given you?

Business Success Tip 21:

After you have done everything that is in the above mentioned tips, **it is time for action**. So it is good to **document** all goals and procedures so anyone can put them into practice even when you are absent. A good business runs by itself.

Business Success **Tip 22:**

Systemise your business so a new staff member can read the manual and run the business. This is also associated with planning so you avoid crisis management. So you **work at the business** not in the business.

Business Success   Tip 23:

It is good to recap how to work at the business not inside the business:

1. Have a goal.

2, Make plans how to achieve the goal.

3. Take action on the plans.

4. Systemise your business.

We can help with all of above as our services are unique or you can do it as well.

Business Success   Tip 24:

If you fail to plan you plan to fail: a business needs plans to be successful otherwise one is doing one crisis management after another and just about surviving with very little income.

There are various type of plans which are essential to run a successful business ie marketing plan, cash flow, budget etc.

<u>Business Success</u>   **<u>Tip 25:</u>**

What happens to businesses who **over promise** and **under deliver**? :
They get a reputation for being unreliable and lose customers.

<u>**Business Success**</u>　　<u>**Tip 26:**</u>

The way to **wow** customers is to **under promise** and **over deliver** and go the extra mile for customers see tip 27. This creates **a wow factor!**

<u>Business Success</u>   **<u>Tip 27:</u>**

Listed below is strong evidence of the **Mighty 10% free**, rule which states give 10% services and goods **free** to your customers:

a. Face book has always given you a lot free. Free social pages, business pages etc: Face book are worth billions:

b. Google have always given a lot free. Free emails, searches and Google documents etc: It is worth billions

c. Hirsch & Co give, free tax planning to business people who come and see us, free advertising on our business success group, free tax and success tips. They have many loyal clients since the last 25 years.

d. We bought a hard drive from Apple with a 12 month warranty. After 18 months it stopped working. They replaced it free immediately although they did not have to. They are worth billions.

So the success tip is **do 10% extra for clients/customers free.**

Business Success  **Tip 28:**

Doing extra free also provides intrinsic rewards for you and is very fulfilling.

Business Success **Tip 29:**

There are **intrinsic** and **extrinsic** rewards. Both are important for success. You get 200% success that way. 100% inner success and 100% outer success.

Intrinsic reward:

Intrinsic reward is the feel good factor and is very satisfying. One gets it when one does something for free. By intrinsic it means form inside one. It is most fulfilling. It is a happy feeling. Poetry, stories, jokes, voluntary work, helping people for free etc give that reward also. It is the intrinsic rewards that make people happy, worthy and fulfilled.

Extrinsic rewards:

Extrinsic rewards are external to you. They are money and material goods and services. They help lead a more comfortable material life. They make you materially secure.

<u>Business Success</u>   **<u>Tip 30:</u>**

Build preference and **differentiation** for your brand over competitors.

Business Success  Tip 31:

Expansion of previous tip:

The best way to beat the recession and also be very successful is by differentiation. By providing **unique goods and services** you can eliminate all competition. Businesses with **unique** products and services are actually growing in this recession. Hirsch & Co provide unique services and hence no other accountant is any competition for them.

<u>Business Success</u>   <u>Tip 32:</u>

Once you have differentiated your service/goods (please see previous tip) by providing **unique** services and goods you have eliminated all competition. You are the King/Queen of the marketplace. Now is the time to think of your target customers.

For examples of unique services and goods, please visit the following website: http://www.hirsch.co.

You can see the web designer, has also done a unique design. One of his web sites has been listed as one of the **best** web sites in **the world**. So he has eliminated all competition for himself. His email is pinnerrd@gmail.com

For examples of goods: Think of BIC ball point pen, Apple computers, Rolls Royce, Marks & Spencer, Sainsbury etc

Business Success   Tip 33:

The following is the **key** to successful marketing and business success so we are repeating it for your benefit. You can spend years studying marketing or you can focus on the following **key elements**:

Once you have **differentiated** your business by providing unique services and goods (In a previous tip we gave examples of how you can easily do this), you have **eliminated** all competition, become the King/Queen of the market place and decided who your target customers are.

Then the next step is to list how you are going to contact them. One of the ways is through this business group http://www.facebook.com/businesuccess. The more people you invite to join this group the more target customers you get free, as it is free to advertise on this group site. There are many other ways listed in **tip 18** given above, but some of them can cost a lot of money. We show you a simple free way of getting business success. In your browser bar type http://www.facebook.com/groups/306912652690200/

For more freebees click the like button on:
http://www.facebook.com/uniqueaccountants
If it does not work copy and paste into the search bar of your browser.

Business Success   Tip 34:

Every business must have a written down **goal**. Running a business without a goal is the same as sailing a ship without a rudder. The 5 year goal should then be broken down into yearly, monthly, weekly and daily goals. This makes daily goals easy to achieve as they are not onerous at all.

Business Success  **Tip 35:**

Have you watched The Fixer on You tube. Here is an expert who goes to businesses and in a very practical way shows them what to do to be more successful.
Please do watch it. It is very practical.
Alex Polizzi: the Fixer.

However one has to adapt the tips for ones own business especially if you are a small business and your customers are price sensitive therefore very posh premises may put them off. They may feel you are too expensive and not for them. Hence, you may actually lose customers. There is no substitute for commonsense.

Unique Accountancy and Taxation Services (just as all business people are not the same all accountants are not the same).

Sole traders and partnership we can save you
at least £3000 in tax over and above what your accountant saves you. This is each year.
Over 10 years this is a saving of at least 30,000. Obviously there should be sufficient profits.

Limited company directors/shareholders we can save you personal tax. For the last 23 years none of our clients have paid any personal tax, car tax etc with our **unique tax planning** which is free for a limited period (based on HMRC rules).

We provide **value** for money **unique** services to you and are **dedicated to saving you money, time and worry.**

Please see the many newspaper articles and testimonials on www.hirsch.co (there is no UK after the .co).
On the web site are listed the 6 unique benefits/services you get from us.

Also type 'Ormskirk accountants' on the Google bar and see more testimonials from well satisfied clients.

We provide Full range of accountancy and taxation services that you may need and tailor make them to suit you.

We also set up Limited companies for you if you need them and deal with all the compliance work both for HMRC and Companies House.

Except for the first introduction, we deal with everything by email thereby saving our clients time and money. Our clients never need to come and see us, only if they want to, for any matter. The first consultation is free.

Distance is no barrier as we use modern technology for communication etc. All paperwork can be posted to us by recorded delivery. That is why we have clients all over North-West of UK, in London, the Middle East and even in China.

We provide free tax and business success tips every Monday for all business people who have given us their email addresses.

Please ring us **NOW** on 01695 578955 for a free telephone consultation.

Email: hirschco@gmail.com

The Kindle version is available for Easy Business Success:
http://www.amazon.com/dp/B00BHADXHO

Is also available in other countries in print:

Amazon United Kingdom - http://www.amazon.co.uk/dp/148418596X

Amazon Germany - http://www.amazon.de/dp/148418596X

Amazon Spain - http://www.amazon.es/dp/148418596X

Amazon France - http://www.amazon.fr/dp/148418596X

Amazon Italy - http://www.amazon.it/dp/148418596X

The audio version will also be out soon on audible:

www.**audible**.co.uk

The Fantastic thriller Sidhaman is also available on Amazon in print and on Kindle. He has a lot of special unique abilities. You will learn about the Golden Age around the corner **for you and your loved ones:**

Print USA
 http://www.amazon.com/dp/1497447453/ref=cm_sw_su_dp

Print UK   http://www.amazon.co.uk/dp/1497447453

Kindle version:
http://www.amazon.com/dp/B00IH10JSW

An audio version will be out soon:
www.**audible**.co.uk
So look forward to more unique books and novels.

Other Great, Best Easy Books on Amazon: Kindle, audio and in print

1. If you have enjoyed the above book, please buy the 'Easy Business Success 2' when it is published by Best Easy Books Ltd via Amazon.

   It shows you how to be more successful in business and jobs in a very practical way. It is very easy to read as I have kept the tips short and simple, as I know busy business people do not have the time to read a lot of stuff. They are easy to practice. Pleas click on:

   The print and audio version will also be available from Amazon Create Space and audible.

If you have enjoyed Easy Business Success:
please put your positive feed back on the above links and print version site and on Harper Collins site:

http://authonomy.com/books/57150/easy-business-success/

2. Other 2 Easy books 'How To Live. 100% of inner, absolute,
   permanent life and 100% of outer, relative life are soon to be published on Amazon.
3. Wait for the 'Book Of Life' also.

Later:

In the next book I will write in detail about 'Sidhaman The Protector' and then in a third book about my many years of experiences with the Mighty Avatars and witnessing many miracles etc. Also will write how their fantastic wisdom can benefit every human being in a big way, to lead a happier and more successful lives. In the fourth book, I will write about my experiences with the Mighty Holy Masters. In the fifth book, about the mighty temples of India.

And many more to look forward to and enjoy: For life is for enjoyment.
   Please tell all your friends, relatives, colleagues, Face book,
   Twitter and other social media friends, about the above-mentioned great books.

I trust this very **unique** book Easy Business Success made very enjoyable, informative reading and gave you lots of intrinsic rewards.

Please email your feedback to
besteasybooks@gmail.com. Your name would be entered in a draw and you could win the book Easy business Success 2 for free as soon as it is published.

For UK taxes you can down load 42 tax tips free on https://www.hirsch.co.

You will also find 5 free offers and 6 Unique benefits for your business on this site.

www.ingramcontent.com/pod-product-compliance
Lightning Source LLC
Chambersburg PA
CBHW071545170526
45166CB00004B/1553